Francisco J. Núñez'

TRANSIENT GLORY

Three Heavens and Hells

Meredith Monk

MEREDITH
MONK
MUSIC

BOOSEY & HAWKES

DISTRIBUTED BY

HAL•LEONARD

COMPOSER'S NOTES

Since 1965, I have been composing music for the voice as an instrument. I've always believed that the voice itself is a language that speaks more eloquently than words. But when my friend Carla Blank, who co-directed the children's dance troupe of Roberts + Blank Dance Theatre, asked me to create music composed to children's poetry I became intrigued by the idea of setting music to text. Carla gave me a book of poems entitled *Electric Chocolate* written by her daughter, Tennessee Reed (whose father is the author Ishmael Reed). I chose "Three Heavens and Hells," written when Tennessee was 11, because it gave me space to work with my own rhythms and phonemes as well as an intriguing set of images to play with. I thought the poem was both whimsical and profound. For example, what would 'Things heaven and hell' be like? I let my imagination fly.

Though originally scored for four female voices, I always envisioned *THREE HEAVENS AND HELLS* being sung by a children's chorus. When the Young People's Chorus of New York City commissioned me, I was excited by the idea of making a new version of the piece. Working with Francisco Núñez and the young singers gave me the opportunity to create different colors and textures, expand my original conception and develop it into a new entity.

THREE HEAVENS AND HELLS may also be performed with an adult chorus of treble voices.

Three Heavens and Hells
by Tennessee Reed

There   are   three   heavens   and   hells

People	Animal	Things
heaven and	heaven and	heaven and
hell	hell	hell

What do the three heavens and hells look like?

They are all the same.

NOTES FOR THE CONDUCTOR

In general, I would like *THREE HEAVENS AND HELLS* to be sung with no vibrato. I would like clear, pure, direct sound. However, if the singers want to add a little vibrato at the end of a phrase for warmth and ease that is fine, but I am definitely going for a crystalline vocal quality.

When a part is marked with "x's" instead of noteheads, it usually indicates a vocal percussion part. When the "x's" are specifically placed on certain lines or spaces on the staff, it means that there is a suggestion of pitch. For example, in "People heaven and hell" I have tried to indicate approximate pitch relationships even though the phrases are not really pitched, but are more spoken than sung. In m. 44 of "Things heaven and hell," Treble 1 performs an unvoiced vocal percussion part (a "kih" sound created by placing the middle of the tongue on the roof of the mouth). At mm. 130-132, there is a section of phonated and unvoiced whispering.

After I had composed *THREE HEAVENS AND HELLS,* images for the piece came to me which may be helpful for the performers. "Animal heaven and hell" begins with a sense of daily events existing in a peaceful place. The parts of Trebles III and IV made me think of a boat going down a river through a rainforest. Those two parts should gently rock. The other parts (solos 1-6 and solo group) are like the fauna and flora of the environment, each inhabitant making itself known gradually. At m. 102, an alien, manmade entity (a bulldozer or a machine or some kind) imposes itself on the place, wreaking havoc. After the onslaught, the survivors establish the quiet rhythm of life once more. In "Things heaven and hell" at mm. 43-58 and 98-128, I imagine inanimate objects ("things") having a life of their own, becoming more and more animated as the movement goes on.

Neither of these scenarios is meant to be literal and are only mentioned here as an aid in finding particular colors or textures in the music. I would hope, particularly for a children's chorus, that these images–only two of many possibilities–would stimulate the singers' imaginations.

Because the vocal sounds in *THREE HEAVENS AND HELLS* are very specific, I strongly suggest that you listen to the examples that I have posted on my website:
www.meredithmonk.org/education/techniques.html.
This will aid in fully understanding the score and singing the piece.

commissioned by
Young People's Chorus of New York City
Francisco J. Núñez, Artistic Director & Founder
for Transient Glory and Radio Radiance
First performed April 13, 2009 at Alice Tully Hall,
Lincoln Center

TABLE OF CONTENTS

for the Young People's Chorus of New York City

THREE HEAVENS AND HELLS

I.

Words by
Tennessee Reed

Music by
Meredith Monk

979-0-051-47998-6

4

II.

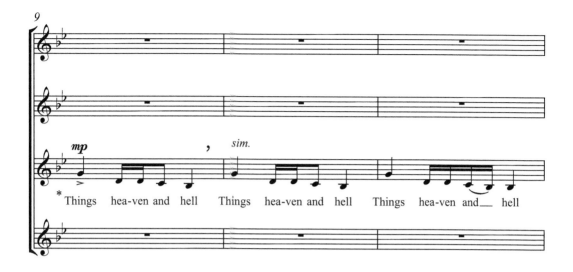

* On the word, "Things" give a strong accent to "th" and go right to "ng"; sustain the "ng," not the vowel.

III.

* More spoken than sung: x-shaped noteheads indicate where in the voice (pitch-wise) the phrase would be spoken.
"G'deh ah-law" is breathy; at the end of "-law" the voice falls off. "Aah" is slightly nasal.

10

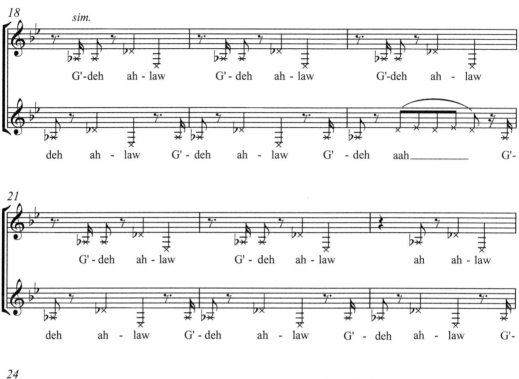

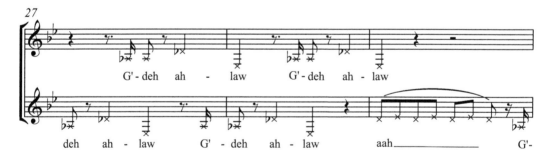

979-0-051-47998-6

979-0-051-47998-6

* Accent "ah" to bring out chromatic differences between the parts.

68
law   G' - deh   G' - deh   ah - -

G' - deh   ah - - law

ah - - law   G' - deh   G' - deh

deh   ah - - law   G' -

69
law G'-deh G'-deh ah - law G'-deh G'-deh ah -

G'-deh ah - law   G'-deh ah - law

ah - law G'- deh G'- deh   ah - law G'-deh G'-deh

deh   ah - law   G' - deh   ah - law   G'-

repeating over and over
* tutti diminuendo - niente
71
law   G' - deh   G' - deh   ah -

G' - deh   ah - law

ah - law   G' - deh   G' -deh

deh   ah - law   G'

* Long diminuendo (ca. 30 measures) with gradually less pitch in the breathy tone to whispers.

979-0-051-47998-6

IV.

* Go straight to the "l" in the final syllable of "animal," thus: "a-ni-ml"; the vowel in "mal" is more like "uh" than "ah."

979-0-051-47998-6

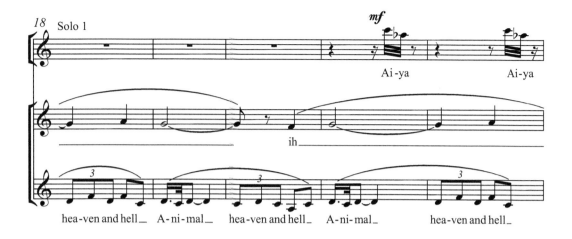

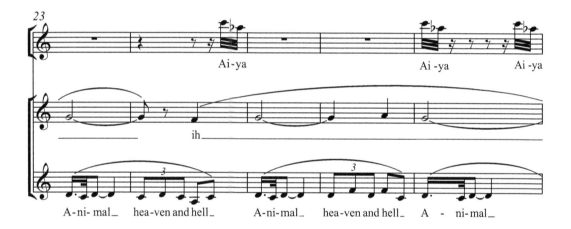

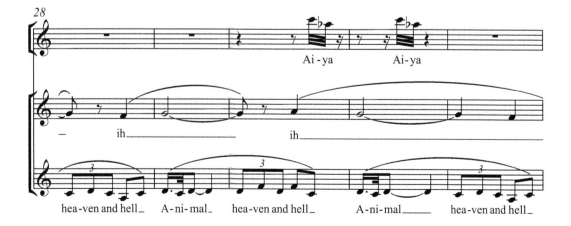

* three voices, no accents

20

* Cross-hatched stems indicate "liga" of "G'liga-lig-ta" should be quickly reiterated. "Ku-i" is pronounced "koo-ee."
Audio examples are available at www.meredithmonk.org/education/techniques.html.

979-0-051-47998-6

* Hollow, dark-sounding, like low wind in the trees. Notation on upper staff indicates pitch and rhythmic contour.

979-0-051-47998-6

ku - i   kui-i   ku - i

G'liga...lig - ta, G'liga...

kay - uh

Solo 6   *f*

*doomh   doomh

_____ ih hih   ih ih __ hih _____ ih _____

hea - ven and hell   A - ni-mal, A - ni-mal hea-ven and hell __ A - ni-mal __

* accented, hard attack

24

animando, poco a poco crescendo

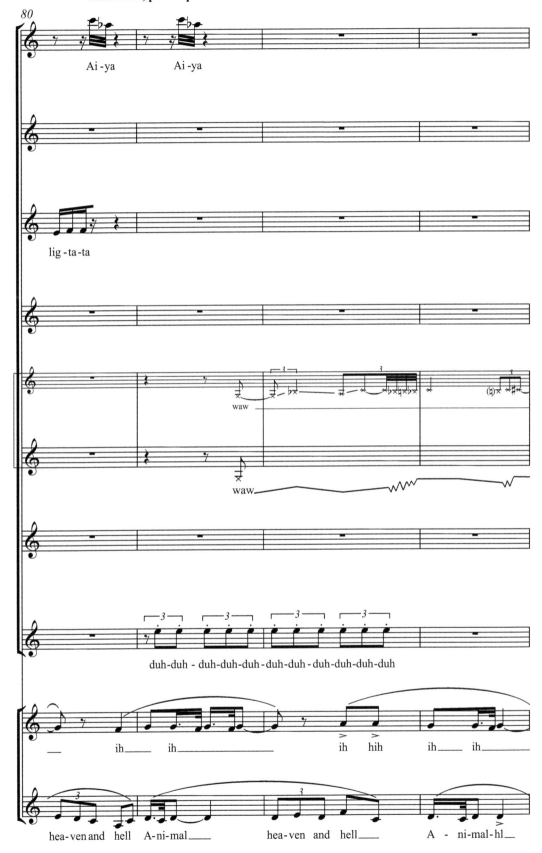

979-0-051-47998-6

91

accelerando, sempre crescendo

979-0-051-47998-6

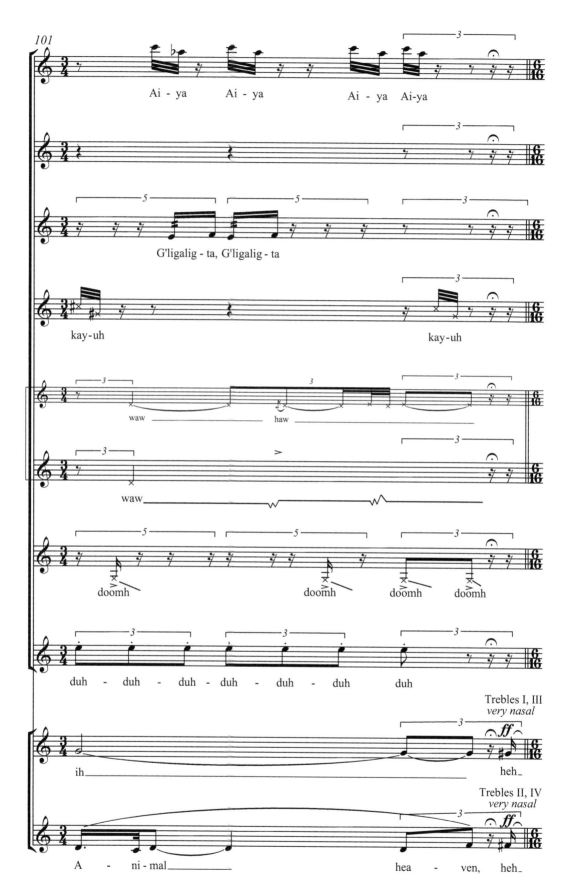

32

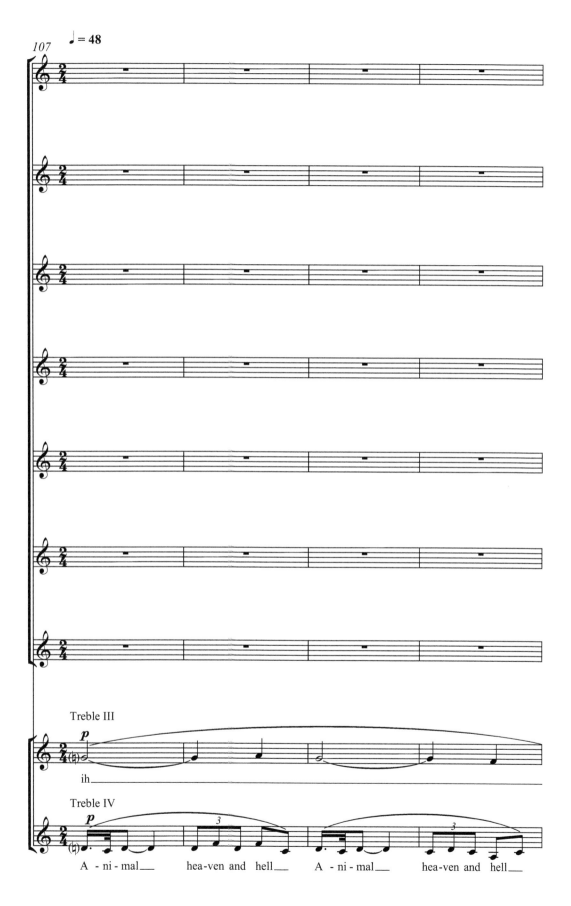

34

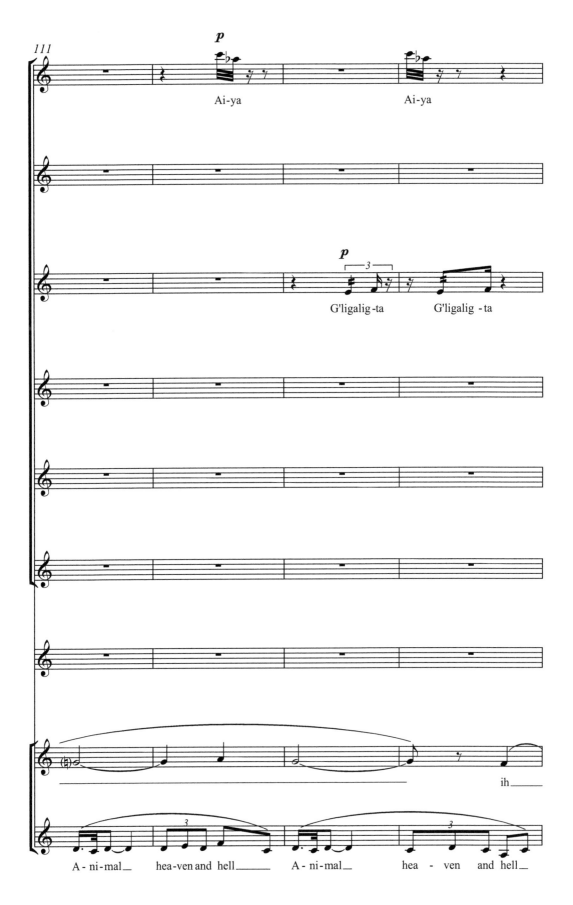

979-0-051-47998-6

36

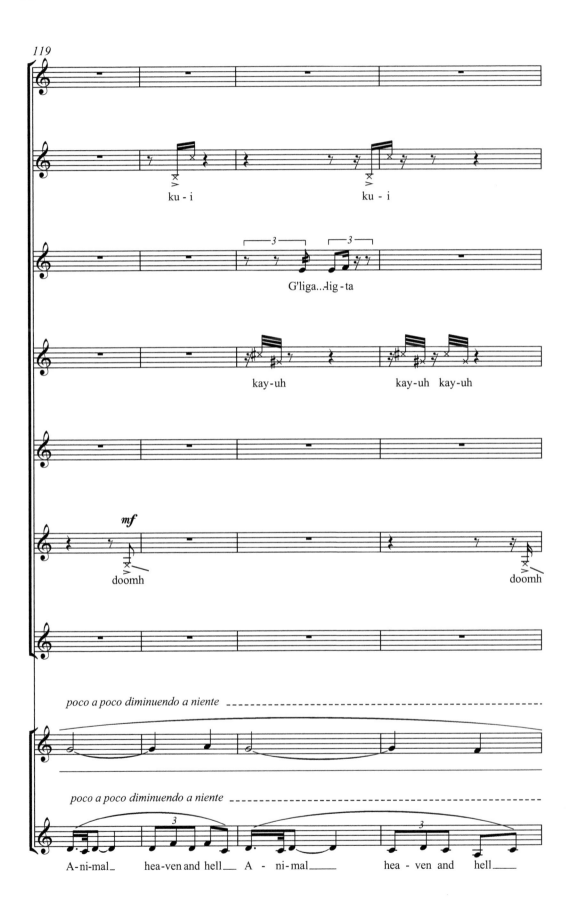

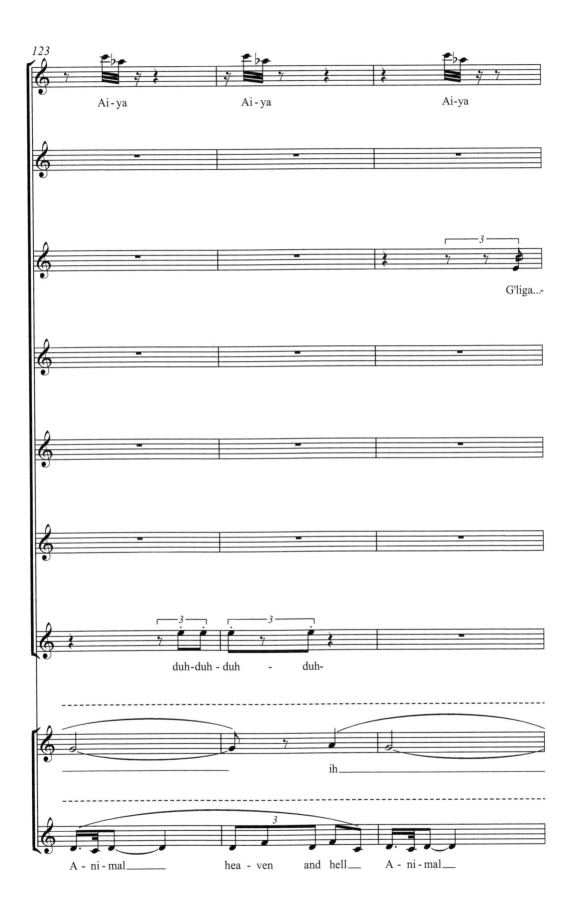

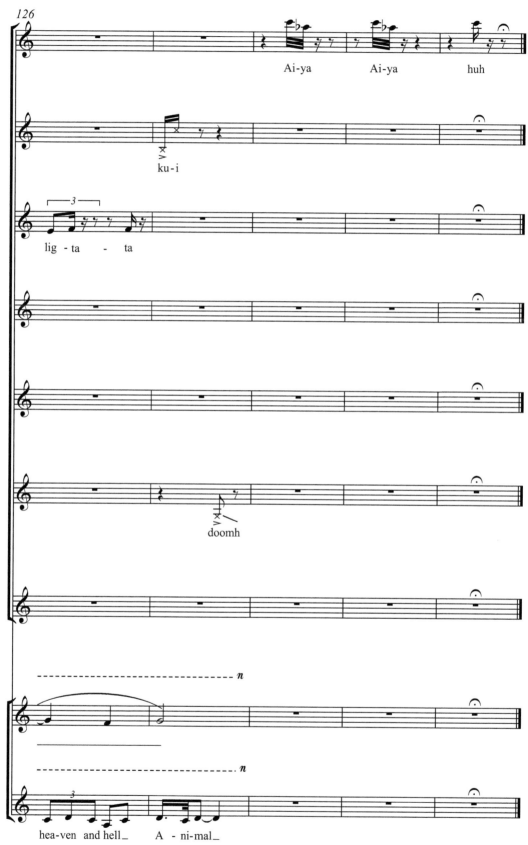

V.

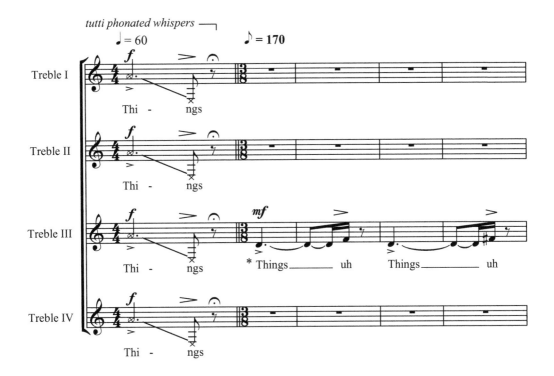

* Tutti give a strong accent on "Th" and sustain the "ng", not the vowel. Treble I, II, IV place the "s" at the end of the sustained note. Treble III carry the "ng" across and place the soft, voiced "s" before "uh", thus "Thing....suh."

979-0-051-47998-6

979-0-051-47998-6

* Solo Group spoken dead-pan with nasal resonance. Solo Group and Trebles should balance dynamically.
  Treble II text continues with "Things" on G naturals and "hea-ven and" or "hea-ven an' uh" on F sharps.

979-0-051-47998-6

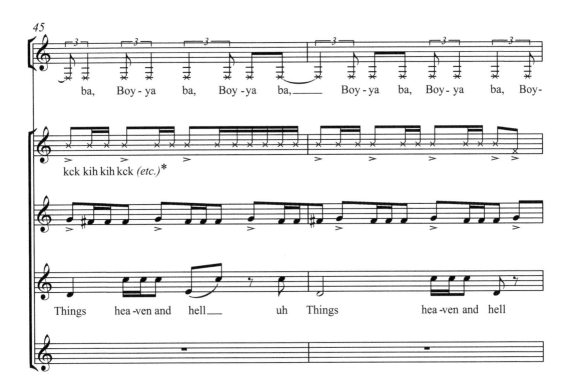

* Treble I continues "kih" on 16th-notes, "kck" on 8th-notes.
  Treble II's "an' uh" becomes "an'-uh nan-uh..." (etc.) as F sharp 16th-note pairs are added.

979-0-051-47998-6

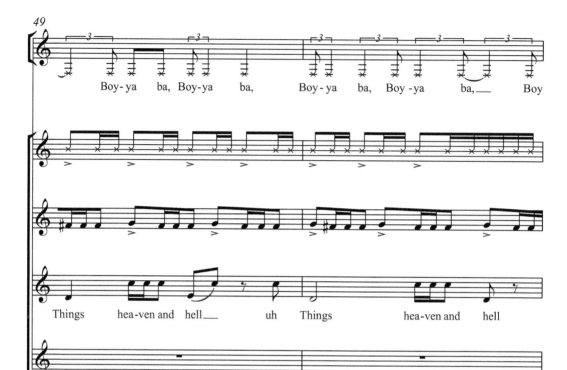

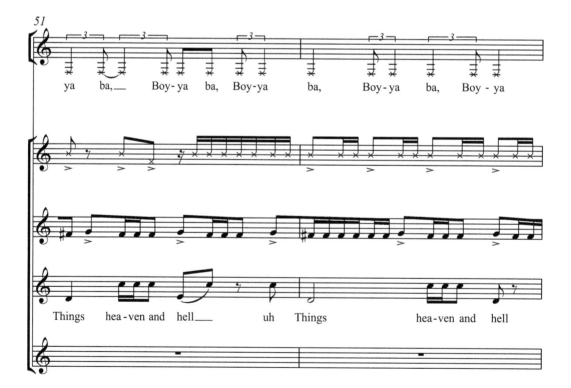

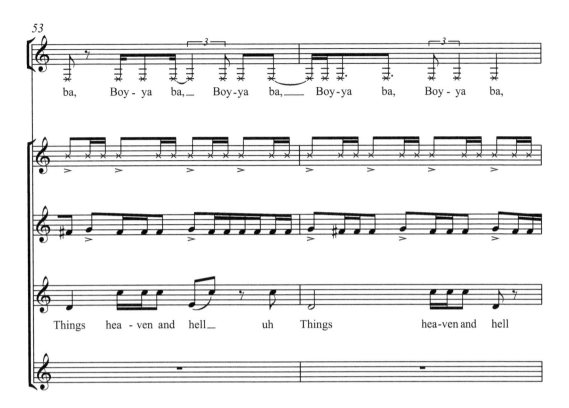

ba, Boy - ya ba,__ Boy-ya ba,__ Boy-ya ba, Boy - ya ba,

Things hea - ven and hell__ uh Things hea-ven and hell

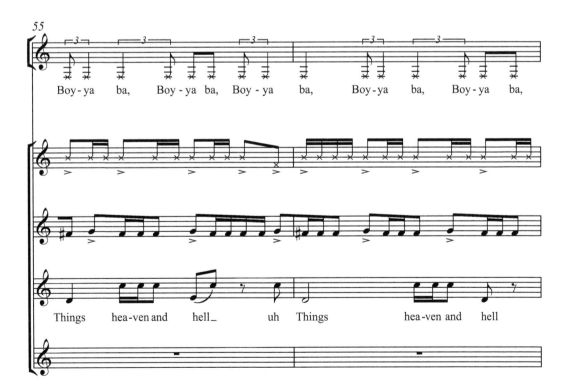

Boy - ya ba, Boy - ya ba, Boy - ya ba, Boy-ya ba, Boy - ya ba,

Things hea - ven and hell__ uh Things hea-ven and hell

979-0-051-47998-6

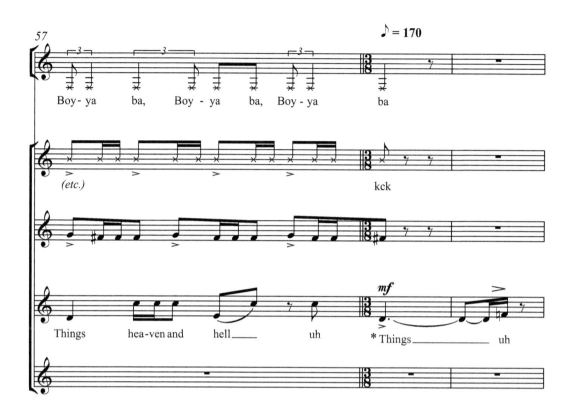

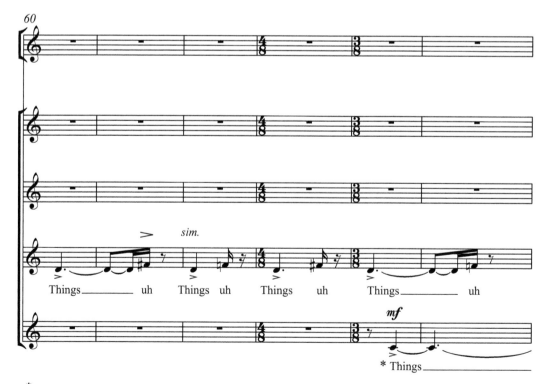

* same instructions as beginning of movement

979-0-051-47998-6

* same instructions as beginning of movement

48

-0-051-47998-6

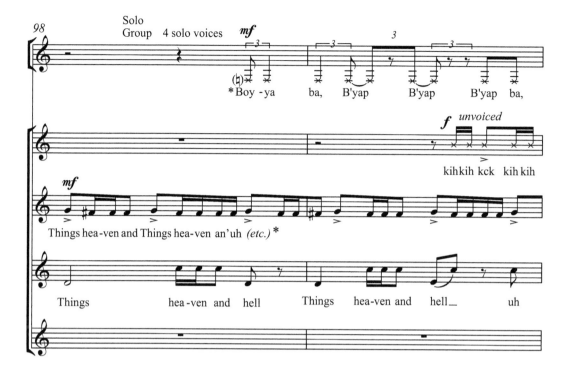

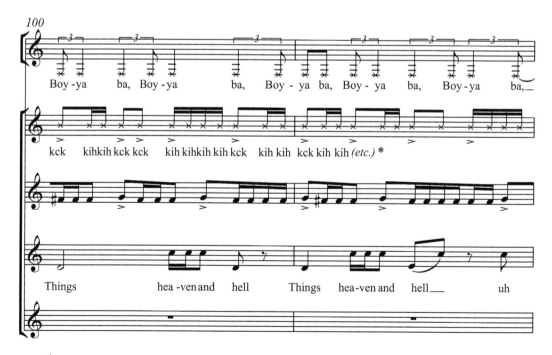

* Same instructions as pp. 42-43.

979-0-051-47998-6

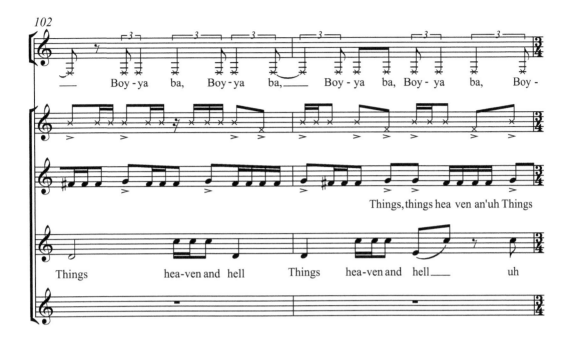

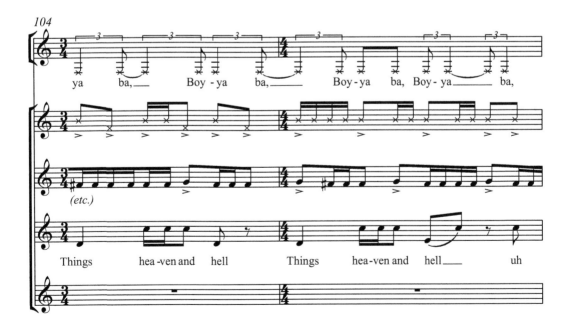

52

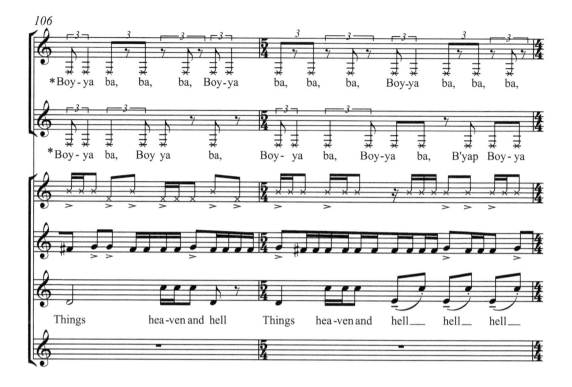

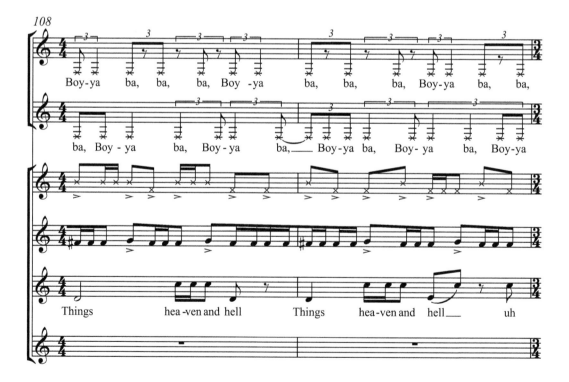

* Solo Group divides: two voices continue on 2nd staff from top and two voices move to top staff.
  Solo Group and Trebles should balance dynamically.

979-0-051-47998-6

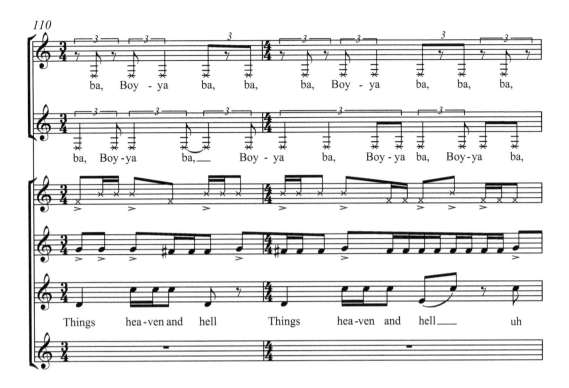

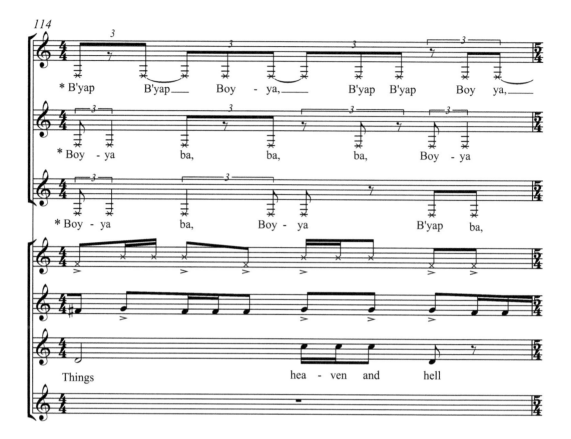

114

115

* Solo Group splits again: two voices continue on 3rd staff from top, one voice continues on 2nd staff from top and one voice moves to top staff.

979-0-051-47998-6

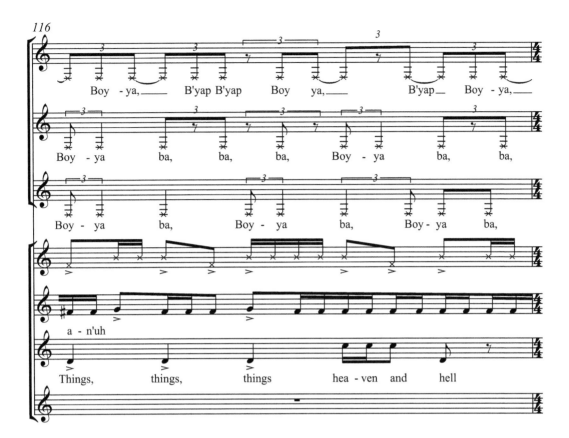

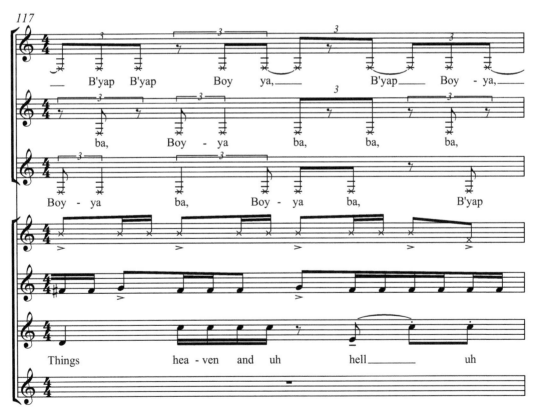

* Treble IV same as Treble II: "kih" on 16th-notes, "kck" on 8th-notes.

979-0-051-47998-6

* Continuing with "Boy-ya-ba" and "B'yap" material, one of the voices on 3rd staff from top begins to improvise based on the written rhythms. This continues until the third beat of m. 128.

979-0-051-47998-6

125

126

979-0-051-47998-6

60

poco a poco diminuendo a niente; 15 seconds

Trebles I-IV

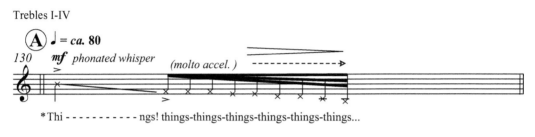

*Thi - - - - - - - - - - - ngs! things-things-things-things-things-things...

Trebles I-IV

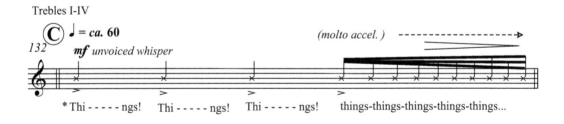

* Things! things, things, things, things things, things, things, things, things, things.

Trebles I-IV

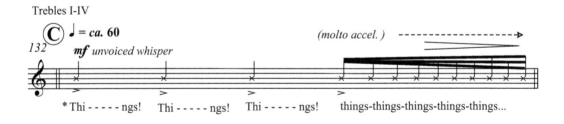

* Thi - - - - - ngs!   Thi - - - - - ngs!   Thi - - - - - ngs!   things-things-things-things-things...

* Tutti chorus. Each individual may choose from among any of the three unmetered measures (A,B,C), repeating them or alternating them. Entrances are up to the individual. The idea is a cascade of sound created by the chorus as a whole. The improvisation continues in this way for 15 seconds, starting medium-loud and gradually fading away to silence.

979-0-051-47998-6

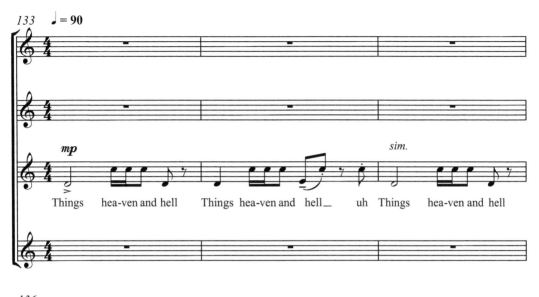

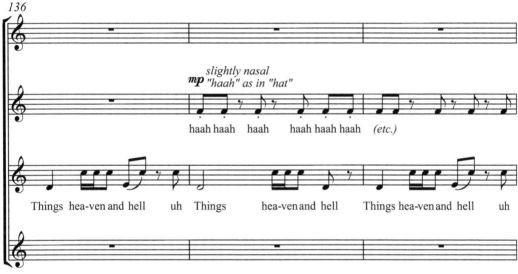

979-0-051-47998-6

142

Things hea-ven and hell__ uh Things hea-ven and hell Things hea-ven and hell__ uh

145

Things hea-ven and hell Things hea-ven and hell__ uh Things hea-ven and hell

148

Things hea-ven and hell__ uh Things hea-ven and hell__ uh Things hea-ven and hell uh

979-0-051-47998-6

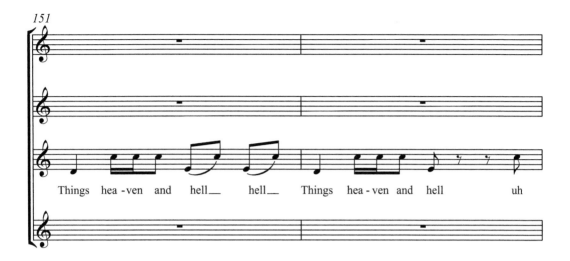

Things hea-ven and hell__ hell__ Things hea-ven and hell uh

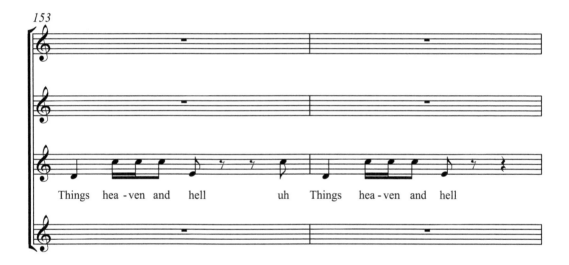

Things hea-ven and hell uh Things hea-ven and hell

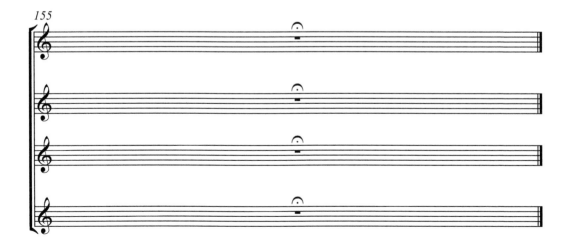

64

VI.

Treble I

Hea-ven hea-ven hea-ven   *hell hell hell hea - ven hea-ven hea-ven

Treble II

Hea-ven hea-ven hea-ven   *hell hell hell hea - ven hea-ven hea-ven

Treble III

Hea-ven hea-ven hea-ven   *hell hell hell hea - ven hea-ven hea-ven

4

hell hell hell hea - ven hea-ven hea-ven   hell hell hell   hea-ven hea-ven

hell hell hell hea - ven hea-ven hea-ven   hell hell hell   hea-ven hea-ven

hell hell hell hea - ven hea-ven hea-ven   hell hell hell   hea-ven hea-ven

8

hell hell hell hea - ven hea-ven hea-ven   hell hell hell hea-

hell hell hell hea - ven hea-ven hea-ven   hell hell hell hea-

hell hell hell hea - ven hea-ven hea-ven   hell hell hell hea-

* At the beginning of the movement the word "hell" is sung; as the dynamic increases "hell" is half-spoken/half-sung.
Let the voice fall off at the end of the word "hell."

979-0-051-47998-6

66

979-0-051-47998-6

979-0-051-47998-6

70

979-0-051-47998-6

VII.

Freely, with dramatic inflection *

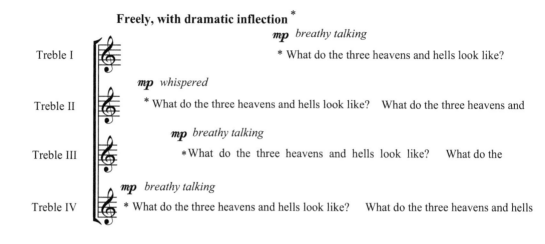

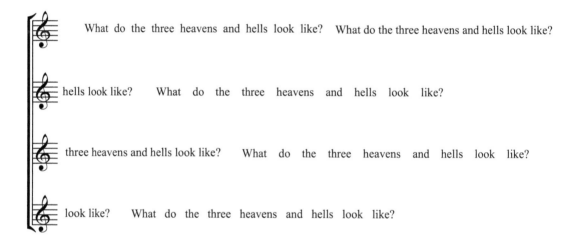

Andante; ♩ = 66

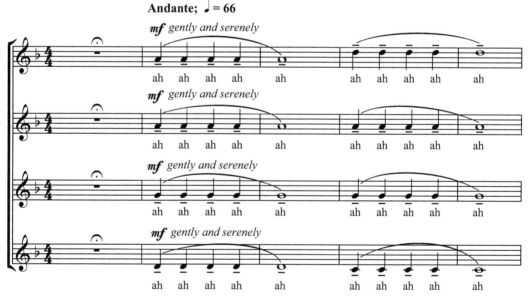

* Each individual asks, "What do the three heavens and hells look like?" three times, emphasizing either the word "what" ("WHAT do the three heavens and hells look like?") or "look" ("What do the three heavens and hells LOOK like?"). The beginning of each question is cued by the conductor but then the individual may decide how to pace and inflect the question.

979-0-051-47998-6